URBINO

A NEW COLOURED GUIDE

Every useful information for the tourist
106 coloured plates - plan of the town

Published and printed by

Narni - Terni
ITALIA

Urbino: an overall view

"Windy Urbino", as Pascoli calls it in a famous poem ("L'aquilone"), is situated on two plateaux overlooking the Metauro and Foglia valleys.

To the approaching visitor, the town presents a proud, severe but coherent appearance, self-enclosed as it is behind its circuit of walls, articulated by a series of bastions.

Rising splendidly over the rooftops of the town is the magnificent Ducal Palace, dominated, even more splendidly and elegantly, by its fairy-tale-like western façade (the "facciata dei Torricini"), defined by its two slender circular towers. The majestic Ducal Palace extends all around, dominating the town. Indeed, the surrounding townscape seems to be so inseparably linked to it as to arouse the sensation of a homogeneous whole, of an urban environment permeated by the same atmosphere such as to justify Urbino's historic definition as a "palace-city".

Urbino has always lived around this wonderful monument, around this "court". Indeed, Urbino is the court itself, having forged with it a communion of cultural and artistic values, dissolved in the process of time without traumas and without upheavals. Its peculiarity, and also its incontrovertible interest and beauty, consists in being a city of art and culture, and at the same time a city of our own day, heightened and enriched as it is by the treasures and history of a splendid past which still confers on it a well-defined character: evocative and self-contained in its medieval townscape, though this is more spacious in scale than that of other towns of the period; splendid, princely and austere in the complex architectural scheme of its Ducal Palace.

Although the various historical periods have left their stamp on the monuments, streets and the townscape itself of the centre of Urbino, and although their signs are everywhere clearly identifiable, Urbino is especially characterized as a creation of the Renaissance.

It is essentially the civilization of the 15th century which harmonizes and fuses Urbino's past. It was it that created — notably by the building of the huge complex of the Ducal Palace — the new face of the town, and that therefore succeeds in determining the homogeneous and highly personalized character which is still peculiar to it to this day and which makes it so unique and so fascinating.

Even the inevitable process of urban development in modern times has left this Renaissance appearance unaltered, since it has been confined to the outlying suburbs and has not intruded into the pre-existing historic nucleus.

Panoramic view.

If Urbino remains one of Italy's most significant and fascinating towns from an historical, artistic and cultural viewpoint, this is because it was the cradle of a splendid Renaissance civilization which had its centre in the court of the ruling Montefeltro family and hence in the Ducal Palace itself, on which converged painters and writers from all over Italy.

It was in Urbino that Raphael, that illustrious Italian painter, was born. Federico Barocci, another distinguished painter (1526-1612), was also born here, and Bramante was born in its environs. It was here, too, that the exquisite art

of majolica was developed, and that one of Italy's oldest universities was founded.

Still today, this profound sense of continuity with the past continues to make itself felt in Urbino. This is not only because the testimonies which have contributed to her fame and splendour have survived unaltered, but also because Urbino has remained a cultural centre of great prestige, as is attested by the many Academies of art, study centres and institutions and manifestations of various kind which attract large numbers of students, scholars, artists and tourists from all over Italy and abroad.

Historical Background

The town almost certainly derives its name from the Latin "Urbs bina", meaning "double town": a name which undoubtedly refers to its situation on two hills.

It was certainly inhabited in prehistoric times and was subsequently a settlement of various Italic peoples. In the Roman period it became a municipium of some importance (known as Urbinum Metaurense), as is attested by the archaeological finds preserved in the Ducal Palace and the few remains of town walls and other buildings of the period.

On the fall of the Roman Empire, it was settled by the Lombards. Then it was annexed to the Byzantine Exarchate, before being restored once again to Lombard rule. It was later incorporated in the Pentapolis (together with Fossombrone, Cagli, Gubbio and Jesi) which was donated to the Church by Charlemagne.

During the Middle Ages it was a Ghibelline (i.e pro-imperial) town: in around 1155 it was assigned by the emperor Frederick Barbarossa to the rule of the Montefeltro family. Ever since then, albeit through a number of vicissitudes and a brief intermission during which it was once again annexed to the Papal State thanks to the exploits of Cardinal Albornoz (1359), Urbino remained, until 1508, in the hands of the Montefeltro family which in a short space of time consolidated its position not only in the military and political field (extending its rule to the neighbouring towns and establishing a powerful duchy), but also in the economic and artistic sphere, turning this little town into a Renaissance court of the greatest prestige, culture and refinement.

It was Federico di Montefeltro (1444-82) who was largely responsible for this great and significant transformation, for it was he who erected the magnificent palace which was to leave its impress so markedly over the whole town, and who turned it, both in size and sumptuousness, into a real court, peopled not only by the ducal family itself, but by the writers and artists that Federico, great patron of the arts that he was, assembled from all over Europe.

In 1508 the duchy of Urbino ceased to be ruled by the Montefeltro family, since Guidobaldo, son of Federico himself, being without heirs, adopted his nephew Francesco Maria, descendent of the powerful family of the Della Rovere. They ruled over Urbino until 1631 when it was definitively annexed to the Papal State; in fact, during the rule of the Della Rovere, the Church had come to exert increasing influence over the political life of the duchy.

The cultural atmosphere which had made Urbino so

splendid under the Montefeltro had long faded. And now the town was even despoiled of so many of the treasures that had lent such brilliance and magnificence to the Ducal Palace: its finest paintings thus came to embellish the courts of Florence and Rome; the decline and fall of this ancient and once glittering duchy was by now inevitable. The history of the town remained linked to that of the Papal State until 1860, when it became part of the Kingdom of Italy.

Today, the town, associated with Pesaro, constitutes one of the provinces of the Region of the Marche.

The town centre and the Ducal Palace

Even though the original town centre of Urbino was formed, in the past, by the Piazza della Repubblica, its most significant nucleus is represented by the Piazza Duca Federico, since it is here that the Ducal Palace stands: the great complex which, from the 15th century onwards, was to become the new and indisputable centre of the town.

Before proceeding, however, to a description of this illustrious monument, let us take a brief look at the other buildings situated in this area, while deferring to a later stage a more detailed account of them.

The Piazza Duca Federico is roughly rectangular in shape. To the south it is prolonged by the adjacent Piazza Rinascimento, one side of which is flanked by a large part of the oldest wing of the palace. Almost at the point of convergence of these two piazzas stands the *Egyptian Obelisk*, a pyramidal column formed of superimposed blocks and carved with hieroglyphs. Donated by Cardinal Albano to the town in the 18th century, it had formerly decorated the front of the Pantheon in Rome.

Facing the Obelisk is the church of San Domenico, while flanking the Palazzo Ducale — rising above a broad flight of steps — is the Cathedral (or *Duomo*).

Both the Piazza Duca Federico and its adjacent Piazza Rinascimento are, however, dominated by the magnificent "winged façade" of the Ducal Palace.

THE DUCAL PALACE

Building history

The Ducal Palace was commissioned by Duke Federico da Montefeltro in the 15th century. It was intended to translate into architectural terms a sense of the importance, power and magnificence achieved by his duchy. Yet in spite of this the building never assumed the appearance

Ducal Palace - Main façade

of a fortress — in contrast to other princely residences of the period — but rather expressed, though in undeniably imposing forms, a sense of elegance, urbanity and composure.

At the start, the task of building it was assigned to the architect Maso di Bartolomeo (c. 1450) who devoted his endeavours especially to remodelling the buildings already existing on the site: in particular he incorporated in the new building the old Palazzo della Jole situated along the

Piazza Rinascimento. A few years later Luciano Laurana was called to Urbino and commissioned to further enlarge the ducal residence. It was he in fact who was the first significant architect of the new palace: he built the parts connecting up with the old "Castellare" (a medieval building situated in the western part of the complex), and designed the ceremonial courtyard and grand staircase, some of the interiors, and especially the wonderful twin-towered "Facciata dei Torricini" — the façade with its loggias looking towards the Appennines — which we shall describe in more detail below.

In 1472 Luciano Laurana left Urbino. Another great Renaissance architect was thus called to complete the work: Francesco di Giorgio Martini, whose genius left a decisive imprint on the town. He brought the palace almost to its completion, drawing his inspiration from his predecessor and substantially respecting his intentions. He devoted his attention especially to defining the decorative features of the façade and to finishing and connecting the pre-existing buildings (such as the "Castellare") with the new nucleus.

In 1482, due to the death of Duke Federico, the building's construction of this great palace was interrupted, even though the main work on it had essentially been completed. It was the architect Girolamo Genga who built the upper part of the palace in the first half of the 16th century.

Subsequently, on the succession of the Della Rovere family and more especially on the subsequent transfer of the town of Urbino to the Papal State, the Ducal Palace was despoiled of a large part of its art treasures. It was only some time after Urbino's annexation to the Kingdom of Italy that this residence, which had by now fallen into a state of abandonment, began gradually to be reclaimed and eventually became, in the early years of the 20th century, the seat of the National Gallery of the Marche.

The restorations to which the palace was subjected from then onwards have been numerous and increasingly better organized. From this point of view, it is worth pointing out the extensive programme of work and study promoted by the Superintendency of the Architectural and Environmental Heritage of the Marche and the Local Authorities in recent years; this has permitted not only the analysis in greater depth of the Building's construction, but more especially the rediscovery of forgotten or concealed parts of it. These latter include, for example the whole extensive complex of cellars and basements comprising bathrooms (including that of Federico himself), kitchens, stables, cisterns and the whole system of water collection, filtering and redistribution, which have recently been reconstructed and opened to the public.

This major programme of restoration and research has thus thrown fresh light on this wonderful palace, extending our knowledge of its structure and adding a series of findings of great interest which especially refer to the aspects of the day-to-day life of the court and to the quotidian experience of the multitude of servants who catered to it.

View of the twin towers. ➤

External tour of the Ducal Palace

The palace presents two façades: the twin-towered façade known as the "Facciata dei Torricini" on the western side and the so-called "winged façade" on the eastern side. The latter, which constitutes the entrance to the palace, faces onto the Piazza Duca Federico and is adorned with elegant, finely sculpted Renaissance portals and eight handsome windows designed by Ambrogio Barocci. A travertine revetment runs along the lower part of the façade, while the rest of the building is in brick.

The palace then extends along one side of the Piazza Rinascimento. This part of the structure, which comprises the ancient Palazzo della Jole incorporated into the rest of the construction by the first architect Maso di Bartolomeo, is characterized by simple but elegant twin-light mullioned windows designed by the afore-mentioned architect.

On reaching the end of the piazza we turn right and join the Via Salvalai, skirting the southern flank of the palace and then reaching its western side, culminating in the "*Facciata dei Torricini*". This undoubtedly represents the most celebrated image of this monument, so much so as to have become its symbol. And with good reason. Due to the incomparable genius of Laurana, this twin-towered façade is a splendid example of Renaissance architecture distinguished by its overall spatial composition, the airiness and elegance of its superimposed loggias and the well-proportioned harmony of its parts. The two tall, slender towers (which have given their name to the façade), projecting out from the main body of the palace, have the function of connecting and containing the structure of the building which had to be adjusted on this side to the marked unevenness of the ground, resting as it does on the steep slope of the hill.

From the "Facciata dei Torricini" we may continue our external tour of the Ducal Palace by ascending a ramp distinguished by the tall buttresses by which it is flanked, and then going up the alleyway known as "Il Giro dei Torricini" which is wedged between the side of the palace and that of the Cathedral, and which brings us back once again into the Piazza Duca Federico.

Interior of the Ducal Palace

The entrance on the left leads into the *Library*. It was once furnished with rare illuminated manuscripts of inestimable value which were transferred to Rome when Urbino was annexed to the Papal State. The Library now houses the State Archives.

To the right of the entrance are the apartments once assigned to the accommodation of guests and to the court theatre; at the present time they house the Institute of Art.

Having explored the outside of the Ducal Palace, we now begin our visit to its interior in which the wonderful *National Gallery of the Marche* is housed.

Through the door to the right of the side of the palace facing the Cathedral, we at first enter the magnificent *Courtyard* (A), a masterpiece of Renaissance architecture designed by Laurana. Surrounded by columned arcades, the courtyard is notable for its harmoniousness, elegance and perfect proportions. The balance and composure of its ensemble, determined by the precise determination of its ideal geometric relations, the exact rhythm of the arches, columns, pilasters and windows, the measured polychromy determined by the alternation of brick and marble, the sense of elegant lightness combined with the rigorous articulation of the architectural lines, everything gives the

Ducal Palace - detail of the courtyard with wiev of the well-bead.

measure of Laurana's classicizing style which has here produced one of the most significant examples of Renaissance art.

The Courtyard consists of a square space with a four-sided portico surmounted by round arches and supported by Corinthian columns running right round it. Along the entablature that runs above the portico's arches there is an inscription praising the exploits of the Duke of Mon-

Ducal Palace - the Courtyard.

tefeltro. In the upper storey, above a slender cornice, is an order of rectangular windows interspersed by pilaster strips. Another inscription runs above the windows, with another projecting cornice above it.

The Latin inscription sculpted in the Courtyard reads as follows: *"Federico Duke of Urbino, Count of Montefeltro and Casteldurante, Gonfalonier of the Holy Roman Church, and Supreme Head of the Italic Confederation,*

raised this residence from its foundations to the glory of himself and his descendents — Federico who went to war more and more times and six times fought and eight times vanquished his enemy, having emerged the victor in all his battles, increased the greatness of his power. Justice, clemency, liberality and religion tempered and embellished his victories in time of peace".

Under the Courtyard's arcades and in the ground-floor rooms adjacent to it is the *Lapidary Museum*, a collection of Roman archaeological finds, inscriptions and seals (currently in the process of being reorganized).

From the Courtyard a monumental *Staircase* (B) of notable proportions designed by Laurana leads up to the upper

Ducal Palace · the main staircase.

floor. This architectural feature of the Ducal Palace is also particularly noteworthy due to the elegance of its plan and its perfect proportions. It consists of three flights of low steps for easy ascent; at the end of the first, we may note the coat of arms of Duke Federico, while a statue of him (sculpted by G. Campagna in the 17th century) is placed on the second landing. The third flight of steps leads up to a beautiful doorway known as the "Porta della Guerra" (Door of War). Adorned with the most delicate friezes and inlays designed by Francesco di Giorgio Martini, it provides access to the room known as the Sala della Jole.

We have now reached the floor of the palace that runs round the Courtyard: here are the rooms that once accom-

The "Porta della Guerra" (Door of War).

modated the Montefeltro court, and which now house the National Gallery of the Marche. This is one of the most significant collections of art in Italy both for the richness and the quality of the works it comprises. Founded in 1912, it has subsequently been enriched and reorganized on several occasions.

The Gallery is displayed on two floors.

FIRST FLOOR

KEY

1 - Sala della Jole
2 - Sala degli Uomini d'arme
3 - Sala dell'Alcova
4ª - Sala
5ª - Sala
6ª - Sala
7ª - Sala
8ª - Sala
9ª - Sala
10ª - Sala
11ª - Sala
12ª - Sala
13 - Sala del Re d'Inghilterra
14ª - Sala
15ª - Sala
16 - Sala delle Udienze
17 - Cappellina di Guidobaldo

18 - Studiolo di Federico
19 - Sala del Guardaroba
20 - Tempietto delle Muse
21 - Cappella del Perdono
22 - Stanza da letto del Duca
23 - Sala degli Angeli
24 - Sala del Trono
25 - Sala delle Veglie
26 - Vestibolo
27 - Salotto della Duchessa
28 - Stanza da letto della Duchessa
29 - Guardaroba della Duchessa
30 - Stànza della Preghiera
A - Cortile d'onore
B - Scalone
C - Scala a chiocciola
D - Loggia

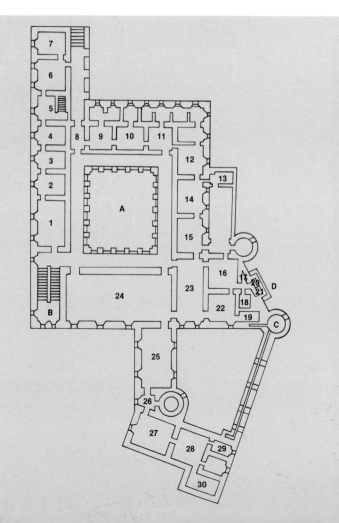

Our visit to the Gallery begings with the

Sala della Jole (1): a room notable for its beautiful fireplace flanked by statues of Hercules and Iole (by Michele da Fiesole).
— fragment of head by Agostino di Duccio
— portraits of the Montefeltro and Sforza families (by Francesco di Giorgio Martini)
— Group of the Madonna and Child with Saints, enamelled terracotta by Lucca della Robbia removed from the façade of the church of San Domenico.
— other sculptural fragments.

Sala degli Uomini d'Arme (Room of Armed Men) (2) with a few remains of somewhat deteriorated frescoes attributed to Giovanni Boccati of Camerino. The frescoes

Fragment of "Annunciation" by Agostino di Duccio (15th century).

The magnificent fireplace of Hercules and Jole.

represent various illustrious men of antiquity.

Sala dell'Alcova (Room of the Alcove) (3): the room takes its name from the beautiful alcove of the Duke of Montefeltro, a work of 15th century woodcarving attributed to Antonio da Camerino. Also on display is a wooden *Cassone* or bridal chest of North Italian manufacture.

Room 4: On display are several works by Giovanni Boccati, including a "Crucifixion" and "Episodes from the Life of St. Sabinus"; by Nicola di Maestro Antonio ("Pietà" and "Annunciation"); a "Crucifixion" by Girolamo di Giovanni and another painting of the same subject by a local Marchigian master.

Room 5: Among others, we may admire the following works:
— "Madonna and Child" by the anonymous artist known as the "Maestro del Boccolo" (15th century)
— polyptych by Andrea di Bartolo di Fredi (14th century)
— various paintings by Marino Angeli.

Room 6-7: Displayed in these rooms are several works by Antonio Alberti of Ferrara, including a fresco of the "Crucifixion" removed from a church. Of particular interest is the sculpture of the "Madonna and Child" attributed to the Florentine artist Lorenzo Ghiberti.

The suite of rooms formerly reserved for the guests of the court now begins.

Room 8: Some detached frescoes dating to the 15th century are here on display.

Room 9:
— Polyptych depicting "The Madonna enthroned flanked by Saints"; dating to 1345, it is the work of the painter Giovanni Baronzio
— "Crucifix" attributed to Pietro da Rimini
— "Crucifix", a work attributed to the so-called Master of

The Duke's alcove.

Main door of the Sala della Jole.

the Crucifix.

Room 10: Particularly noteworthy in this room is the elegant fireplace that decorates it. Two works by the so-called Master of the Coronation of the Virgin, a name derived from the title of his most famous work, are on display here. The other of his paintings represents the "Crucifixion".

Room 11:
— "Madonna and Child" by Allegretto Nuzi (14th century)
— "Madonna del Latte" by Master Antonio
— "Saint Clare" attributed to Salimbeni
— "Annunciation" by C. Del Carmine
— "Madonna and Child", a work by an unidentified Marchigian painter of the 15th century.

23

Portrait of Battista Sforza (Federico da Montefeltro's wife) by Piero della Francesca (1466) · Florence: Uffizi Gallery.

Room 12: It contains among other works the statue of the "Madonna and Child" and the group of the "Annunciation", as well as a "Madonna of Mercy" by an anonymous 15th century master of the Marchigian school.

Room of the King of England (13), so called because it once accommodated (in the 18th century) the self-styled James III, Stuart claimant to the throne of England. The room is distinguished by its beautiful ceiling with stucco friezes produced by Federico Brandani.

Portrait of Federico da Montefeltro by Piero della Francesca (1466) · Florence: Uffizi Gallery.

Room 14: Among the works on display here we may especially note:
— "St. James", two paintings of the same subject by Carlo Crivelli
— works by G. Antonio da Pesaro, Pietro Alemanno and Lorenzo d'Alessandro.

Room 15: Of the paintings preserved in this room we may especially point out one of the masterpieces of the 15th century Venetian master Giovanni Bellini, the "Holy

Audience Hall.

Family". A polyptych by Alvise Vivarini and paintings by Mansueti, Girolamo Santocroce and Marco Basaiti are also on display.

At this point the apartament reserved for guests ends and the apartment of Duke Federico begins.

Audience Hall (16)The room is dominated by its great fireplace, but what especially draws the visitor's attention are the two wonderful masterpieces by Piero della Francesca: the "Flagellation" and the "Madonna and Child" known as the "Senigallia Madonna". We are here confronted by two real jewels of the art of the 15th century which in the hands

of this artist reached some of its highest attainments. In
these and other of his paintings he wonderfully embodied
the new acquisitions and trends of the vast cultural and
artistic movement we now know as the Renaissance. The
mathematical exactness of the perspective, the rigorous
precision of the spatial relationships, and the realism and
substance of the figures, are the expression of man who
has conquered a new dimension, who finds himself in a
reality of his own that is measurable and tangible, and
who thus makes himself lord and master of the world that
surrounds him.

About the interpretation and meaning of the first of these

"The Flagellation of Christ" by Piero della Francesca.

paintings there has been a great deal of discussion among art historians: some have seen in it a comparison between the fate of Christ and that of Oddantonio di Montefeltro (the fair-haired young man in the foreground), the brother of the Duke killed in a plot; others have seen in it a more subtle symbolism which interprets the flagellation of Jesus as the decadence of the Church and the fair-haired young man as the son of Federico da Montefeltro flanked by Cardinal Bessarion (the presumed commissioner of the work) who is trying to convince the Duke to take part in a crusade to resolve the fate of the Church itself.

The other painting by Piero della Francesca, the "Senigallia Madonna", is particularly interesting for its subtle chromaticism: this consists of a limited range of rather pale colours, but an important role in the painting is played by the light filtering through the half-closed window behind the Madonna's back. Striking, too, is the apparent solidity of the figures and also the familiarity of the two angels by whom the Madonna and Child are flanked; these seem to have been divested of every otherwordly or mystical aspect, firmly related as they are to the tangible and almost domestic space in which the painting is set.

"The Senigallia Madonna" by Piero della Francesca.

Chapel of Guidobaldo (17): This tiny chapel, built for Guidobaldo II Della Rovere, is notable for its ceiling vault magnificently decorated with stuccoes by Federico Brandani. The painting of the "Madonna and Saints" on its altar is by an unknown Marchigian painter (16th century).

We now enter one of the most evocative rooms in the Ducal Palace, to the decoration of which some of the most illustrious artists of the time contributed, including Baccio Pontelli, Bramante and Botticelli:

Federico's Study (18): The lower surfaces of the walls of this small room (the *Studiolo*) are completely covered by panels of elaborately inlaid wood. The various intarsias by which they are decorated represent books, shelves, musical instruments and other objects, and allegorical figures, portrayed according to the strict laws of perspective.

Above, a series of portraits of famous men are arranged; the missing ones were long since transferred to other galleries, notably the Louvre in Paris.

Garde-Robe (19): This small room is notable for its elegant fireplace and a tapestry strip illustrating the hunt.

We then descend a spiral staircase (C) contained within one of the two cylindrical towers of the western façade. This leads to two small but fascinating chambers. The first of these, reached through a small vestibule, is the

Temple of the Muses (20), with a charmingly decorated barrel-vaulted ceiling, but with its walls now despoiled of the paintings that once decorated them.

Cappella del Perdono (Chapel of Forgiveness) (21): adjacent to it is this wonderful little chapel. Lavishly faced in precious marbles, it has a barrel vault decorated with stucco heads of angels. Its architectural design has been attributed to Bramante.

Before re-ascending to the upper floor, we should step out onto the loggia or balcony (D) to enjoy the magnificent

Duke Federico's study (the Studiolo).

Detail of the Duke's study.

panoramic views over the town and the landscape beyond. We then return to the Garde-Robe (19), before making our way to the

Duke's Bedroom (22), adorned with a handsome fireplace with gilded friezes. On the walls:
— "Portrait of Duke Federico" by Pedro Barreguete
— "Madonna and Child" of the school of Verrocchio.

Room of the Angels (23) This is one of the largest and finest rooms in the palace. Especially magnificent is its
— fireplace, sculpted by Domenico Rosselli in the 15th century and adorned with a frieze of stone polychrome cherubs (whence the room's name);
— 2 doors: magnificently inlaid with representations of architectural perspectives or mythological figures. The designs for these were probably produced by Francesco di Giorgio Martini, but a number of art historians are increasingly arguing for an attribution to Botticelli. It should be noted here that all the doors of the palace are par-

The Cappella del Perdono (Chapel of Forgiveness).

Temple of the Muses.

ticularly striking either for their superbly sculpted marble mouldings or for their wooden inlays.

— "Madonna and Child" (*gesso* of Marchigian art)
— "Madonna and Child" (*gesso* attributed to Domenico Rosselli)
— "Communion of the Apostles", large painting by Giusto di Gand (Justus of Ghent)
— "Madonna and Child", marble bas-relief by Tommaso Fiamberti
— "The Ideal City", by Luciano Laurana. This is one of the most significant and famous paintings of the 15th century in Italy, since it consists of a pictorial version of the urbanistic conception developed during the Renaissance.
— "The Profanation of the Host" by Paolo Uccello. This consists of a long narrow painted panel (a predella, or lower panel for an altarpiece), divided into six consecutive scenes — recounting a miracle of the Host — which are striking for their narrative freshness and immediacy.

From the Room of the Angels we make our way into the

Throne Room (24): As the name suggests, this was the room in which Duke Federico received his court. Of notable dimensions, the hall is spacious, luminous and solemn, though at the same time characterized by its extreme simplicity. It has two handsame fireplaces and a vaulted ceiling decorated with rosettes.On the far wall is a bas-relief representing the Lion of St. Mark (Guidobaldo I was Captain of Venice). The other walls are hung with a series of Gobelins tapestries (17th century), produced as copies of others based on cartoons by Raphael (representing the "Lives of the Apostles").

The Apartment of the Duchess, installed in the rooms that formerly belonged to the medieval building of the Castellare, now begins.

The Duke's bedroom.

Portrait of Duke Federico and his son Guidobaldo.

Room of the Musical Gatherings (25), so called because it was here that "The group of gentlemen and artists commemorated by Baldassarre Castiglione in his book "The Courtier" used to meet. A number of works by Giovanni Santi (the father of Raphael) are assembled in this room: "Polyptych", "Dead Christ", "Martyrdom of St. Sebastian", "St. Roch", the Archangel and the young Tobias" (divided into two panels), "St. Regina Martyr", "Pietà" and "Madonna and Child" (fresco removed from a church).

Two paintings by Luca Signorelli are also displayed in this room: a "Crucifixion" and the "Descent of the Holy Spirit". Two fine bas-reliefs by Tommaso Fiamberti may also be noted.

The Sala degli Angeli - Door attributed to Domenico Rosselli.

Vestibule (26), small passageway where a door, now closed up, gave access to the spiral staircase.
— "St. Sebastian", by Timoteo Viti
— profile of emperor crowned with laurel wreath (Florentine school of the 15th century)
— stained glass, also designed by Timoteo Viti.

The Sala degli Angeli · Fireplace.

Sala degli Angeli · "The Profanation of the Host" by Pao-lo Uccello: A merchant receives a consecrated host from a woman in payment.

He attempts to destroy it by placing it on the fire.

In an expiatory procession and rite, the host is restored to the altar.

The repentant woman is condemned to be hanged.

The merchant and his family are burned at the stake.

The final scene: angels and devils contend for the woman's soul while her corpse lies on its bier.

Salon of the Duchess (27):
— "St. Sebastian" by Pedro Barreguete
— "Christ giving his Blessing", perhaps by Bramantin but attributed by others to Melozzo da Forlì. Though in part damaged, this is a wonderful and highly expressive painting.
— "Portrait of a Gentlewoman", a famous painting by

Portrait of a Gentlewoman knows as "La Muta" by Raphael.

Wooden "Annunciation" by Carlo da Camerino.

Raphael, characterized by its extreme gentleness and reminiscences of Leonardo da Vinci.
— Statue of the Madonna, by Torrigiano.
— Group of works by Timoteo Viti ("Mary Magdalen", "St. Apollonia", "The Trinity", "St. Thomas and St. Martin").
   We now pass through a magnificent doorway — the "Door of War" as it is called — richly decorated with bas-reliefs and intarsias, and enter the

   Bedroom of the Duchess (28): apart from tapestries and paintings by Raffaellino del Colle ("Madonna of Succour") and Vincenzo Pagani ("Annunciation"), this room contains

"The Ideal City" by Luciano Laurana.

two interesting works by Titian. Depicting "The Last Supper" and "The Resurrection", they were actually painted to serve as standards.

At the end of the room two doors lead into small rooms:

Garde-robe of the Duchess (29), a room linked to the Duke's apartment by an internal passageway. Its walls are decorated with paintings by Pellegrino Tibaldi and Federico Zuccari.

Throne Room decorated with tapestries.

Throne Room · Tapestry: "The Handing Over of the Keys"

Prayer Room (30): striking for its beautiful ceiling with decorations by Federico Brandani.

We then return to the Throne Room, where our visit to the rooms on this floor of the palace ends.

Throne Room-Tapestry: "Blinding of the Magician Elima".

The Sale delle Veglie (Room of the Musical Gatherings).

Throne Room · Tapestry: "The Miraculous Draught of Fish".

The Sala delle Veglie (Room of the Musical Gatherings):
"Madonna and Saints" (Sacra Conversazione)
by Giovanni Bellini

SECOND FLOOR

As we already have had occasion to point out in connection with the building of the Ducal Palace, this second floor was erected during a later period. In fact, the princely Montefeltro residence conceived by the genius of Laurana was originally intended to consist of only one storey and to be topped by a handsome crenellated roofline which was to make it resemble, in some way, an ancient castle. This crenellation is still in part visible today, since it is distinguishable in brick, incorporated into the upper storey's external wall.

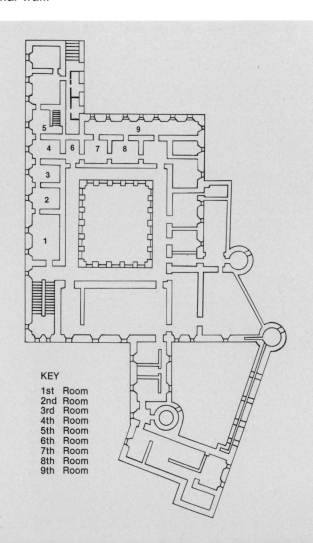

KEY

1st Room
2nd Room
3rd Room
4th Room
5th Room
6th Room
7th Room
8th Room
9th Room

The second floor was therefore added later. It was commissioned by the Duke Guidobaldo II della Rovere (as may be observed by the frequent repetition of his device in many of its rooms). It was he who, in the first half of the 16th century, entrusted its design and execution to the architect Bartolomeo Genga. Genga did nothing but repeat the same scheme and the same style as the pre-existing building. But the palace's general appearance and overall proportion and effect were altered as a result of the doubling of its floors.

Today many scholars agree in maintaining that Duke Federico da Montefeltro himself did have the intention to enlarge his residence by the addition of a second storey. This is indeed inferred by the presence of his initials "F.D." at the beginning of the second flight of stairs which gives access to the upper floor.

Recently, various rooms on this floor have been opened to the public (previously, only the two rooms containing the collection of ceramics could be visited). Paintings by Federico Barocci and other artists of the 17th and 18th centuries have now been arranged in these rooms, which are entirely decorated by Federico Brandani.

1st Room: consists of the large entrance hall and is also known as the Barocci Room because it contains many works by this famous native-born artist. He was born in Urbino in c. 1530-35 and died here in 1612. Strongly influenced by the painting of Raphael and in part by that of the Venetian school and Correggio, he was one of the most significant exponents of Italian Mannerism in the late 16th century. His preferred subjects were religious, and in this he was strongly influenced by the Counter Reformation — as is attested by the collection of his works on display in this Gallery, as well as by other of his paintings held in important museum collections both in Italy and abroad.

A distinguishing feature of his art is his delicate use of colour and light which lends gracefulness to all his compositions and confers a sense of balance and spaciousness on them, even when they are complex in structure.

Of the paintings on display in this first room we may mention in particular:
— "The Crucifixion"
— "The Assumption"
— "Madonna and Child", a particularly well-balanced and composed word.

"The Assumption" by Federico Barocci. ➤

*"Madonna and Child with Saints Simon and Jude"
by Federico Barocci.*

"St. Francis receiving the Stigmata" by Federico Barocci. ⮞

— "St. Francis receiving the Stigmata", one of Barocci's justly most famous and interesting paintings. Note in particular the effect created by the play of light on the details of the representation.

"Annunciation" by a pupil of Barocci.

"The Three Goals".

2nd Room: here we may admire other works by Barocci and his pupils and followers, such as a beautiful "Annunciation". Noteworthy too is the striking pictorial decoration of the room. It represents the "Three Goals": in particular, three cones by which Duke Guidobaldo wished to symbolise the achievement of three objectives: Faith in God, the Continuity of the Kingdom and the Perfect Government.

3rd Room: the room is notable for its fine, richly decorated fireplace, sculpted by Federico Brandani.

Among the works of art on display, of particular interest are the paintings of Orazio Gentileschi, a Tuscan painter and exponent of the late Mannerist style who was influenced by Caravaggio. He is represented by a "Madonna and Child" (17th century). Another painter worthy of note is Simone de Magistris, who is also represented by an altarpiece of the "Madonna and Child".

4th Room: here we find works by Benedetto Marini, a painter of Urbino who lived between the late 16th and early 17th century, and Claudio Ridolfi, who is represented by:
— "The Presentation of the Virgin"
— "The Birth of John the Baptist"
— "The Assumption"
Mention should also be made of Pomarancio's fine "Madonna and Child".

5th Room: it contains works by followers of Barocci. Noteworthy too is the statue of St. Crescentino, a saint much loved in Urbino and indeed the town's Protector.
Various portraits of illustrious men are also displayed in this room, including a self-portrait of Barocci.
The ceiling of the room is adorned with a large and beautiful Eagle: the symbol of the house of Montefeltro.
The rooms that follow, only recently opened, have been created by the closing-up of the terraces.

6th Room: (or passage-way). It is hung with monochrome paintings by Claudio Ridolfi representing "Scenes from the Life of St. Paul".

Firplace by Federico Brandani.

"Madonna and Child" by Orazio Gentileschi.

"The Presentation of the Virgin" by Claudio Ridolfi.

7th Room: 15th and 16th century paintings by Antonio da Pesaro, Bartolomeo di Mastro Gentile and others are displayed in this room.

Also noteworthy here are various drawings and prints by Barocci himself and his pupils, and a charcoal drawing by Annibale Caracci representing "Bacchus and Ariadne".

In the same room is displayed a large "Polyptych" of Giovanni Antonio da Pesaro in which the fine representation of the Madonna and Child is especially striking.

"Madonna and Child" by Pomarancio.

Self-Protrait by Federico Barocci.

Room with paintings representing the Life of St. Paul.

The Eagle: symbol of the Dukes of Montefeltro.

Statue of St. Crescentino by Camillo Mariani.

Polyptych by Giovanni Antonio da Pesaro.

8th Room: the collections of ceramics from various Marchigian potteries have been assembled in this room; they include some wonderful examples of an art which has very long traditions in this region and testifies to its centuries-old cultural ferment. We may mention in particular the magnicifent majolicas from Faenza, Pesaro and Urbino, just to cite the major centres of production. The pieces of pottery displayed in this room are numerous and many of them deserve to be discussed in greater detail. Conspicuous among them is a large majolica formed of 4 panels representing "St. George Killing the Dragon", a theme dear to the artists of the past and inseparably linked to the history of the town.

We may also mention a beautiful representation of the "Nativity" and the distinguished and valuable collection of vases, all of them characterized by their elegant and elaborate decoration.

9th Room: this room, which is like a gallery in structure, was formed by blocking up a terrace that served as a lookout and faced onto the underlying Giardino del Pasquino.

"St. George killing the Dragon".

"The Nativity".　　　　　　*Collection of ceramics.* ➤

Along its external walls are still visible the merlons that constituted the Palazzo Ducale's crenellated roofline before it was raised a storey in height; the pre-existing crenellation can be identified — in relation to the wall surface — by its brick construction. The room commemorates the nuptials of Duke Federico Ubaldo della Rovere and Claudia dei Medici in the form of 17 interesting paintings that cele-

brate the important event (1621) and that represent salient moments and leading personages in the ceremony. They were painted in monochrome by Girolamo Cialdieri and Claudio Ridolfi.

Noteworthy too are the interesting "grotesques" that ornament part of the ceiling. "Grotesques" are a highly original and fanciful form of mural decoration that characterized much of.   Renaissance and post-Renaissance art: they consist of a combination of lines, interlacing, volutes, arabesques, human forms, floral ornaments and other strange motifs invented by the ever-new fantasy of the decorator. They derived their inspiration from pictorial ornamentation of the Roman period found in such buildings as the Golden House of Nero during archaeological excavations in the early 16th century.

Celebration of the Nuptials of Federico Ubaldo della Rovere and Claudia dei Medici.

Ceiling with grotesque decorations.

On leaving the National Gallery of the Marche, we go back down to the Courtyard on the ground floor. From here, through a large portal situated under the portico to the right of the ticket office, it is possible to go down into the *Cellars* of the Ducal Palace. These consist of a huge complex of rooms which have only recently been opened

Wine Cellar.

to the public, thanks to a long-term programme of work and restoration aimed at the rehabilitation of this part of the palace in recent years. The studies and research so far carried out (others have still to be completed) have permitted the elucidation not only of aspects of court life that had remained largely forgotten, but also technical features

Bathroom of the Duchess.

concerning the structure of the building, the hydraulic and hygienic system and the organization of ancillary services. We may note the elaborate system of pipes with which the palace was equipped: linked to cisterns and wells, they re-distributed the water, after appropriate filtering, to the kitchens and bathrooms. We may also inspect the complex of kitchens themselves and bathrooms (especially that of Duke Federico), equipped with hot water thanks to a simple but effective system of heating by fireplaces and braziers and by a more sophisticated system of double walls which enabled the temperature of the rooms to be controlled.

A permanent exhibition based on explanatory panels

has also been mounted in the Cellars. It explains the essence of the history of Urbino and more particulary the history of the Ducal Palace with essential references to the different phases in its construction, the connection between it and the pre-existing buildings on the site, and the function played by the various sectors of the palace in successive periods in its history. Moreover, the materials found during the excavations carried out in this area have been appropriately assembled in display cases and catalogued. They consist for the most part of objects and articles associated with the complex of kitchens and bathrooms situated here. But there are also fragments of statues and sherds of Roman potterly which testify to the presence of buildings of the Roman period in this part of Urbino.

At the lowest level of the Cellars are the storerooms and stables. These were directly linked with the interior of the palace by a staircase located in one of the circular towers.

Let us now look in more detail at the huge complex of the Cellars. From the courtyard of the Ducal Palace a large portal admits to a broad ramp which leads down to a spacious chamber in which the Laundry was once situated. Here all the cloth and dresses for the Court were treated, dyed and washed.

A small room to the left is furnished with a large basin which had the function of storing snow. It was in effect a primitive refrigerator used for the conservation of food and meat: a system which reflects the ingenuity and modernity of our ancient forefathers.

Other rooms adjacent to the laundry were assigned to various domestic services. In one of them, for example, was located one of the cisterns we have already mentioned; this had the job of collecting and then distributing water to the whole palace by means of a functional system of pipes. The water was first filtered to ensure that it was purified and suitable for drinking.

Round these rooms stretch two large chambers: in the first, horses were groomed and saddled, while in the second they were stabled. To the side of the stalls is a long and broad flight of stairs by which the Duke and Duchess could descend without having to leave the palace; in fact it provides direct communication between their Apartments and the Cellars. We may also note the apertures in the floor of the stalls by which the animals' swill was drained away.

Beyond this first group of rooms and on the other side of the central corridor, a series of other services were laid out. They included latrines for the servants, stablemen and cooks; dressing-rooms, pantries, kitchens, woodstores, wine cellars, etc. Here we may also see the Duke's bathroom which, in structure, re-evokes the plan of bathhouses of the Roman period. We may then note the large fireplace situated next to the large central kitchen.

As may be seen in the course of a visit to the Cellars, everything was perfectly organized and planned with maximum efficiency. Indeed, it is possible to see how this huge complex of rooms situated below the residential quarters of the Ducal Palace itself contributed to maintain the tone, and cater to the needs, of the magnificent prin-

Corridor of the cellars.

Wash-house and dye-house for wool.

cely life lived on the upper floors.

The Cellars represent an exceptional example of efficiency and modernity. The services they comprised, so varied and functional in operation, were really ahead of their time.

Library of the Duke - Ceiling

On leaving the Courtyard of the Ducal Palace, we find to the right the entrance to the Duke's Library.

It was furnished with manuscripts and books and documents of the greatest importance which were transferred to the Library of the Papal State (what is now the Vatican Library) after Urbino was annexed to the territories of the Roman Church. At the present time, it houses the State Archives, they two enriched with books and documents of considerable value.

We may note the beautiful ceiling decorated with the coat of arms of Duke Federico da Montefeltro: an eagle placed amid a radiant sun.

Archaeological Museum of Urbino

The Archaeological Museum was inaugurated in 1756 by Cardinal Legate Giovan Francesco Stoppani, with the aim of permitting the display and study of the finds (mainly inscriptions) collected by Monsignor Raffaele Fabretti. The latter had been given the task (in c. 1688) of recovering and preserving the relics contained in ancient sacred cemeteries. As a result of this venture and the vast erudition he displayed in other fields of knowledge, Monsignor Fabretti (a native of Urbino) won great renown among the learned in the 17th century. Cardinal Stoppani for his part had the great merit of seeing to it that this collection was arranged and displayed in a worthy manner. He also enriched it with new finds, turning it into the largest collection then to be seen outside Rome. As a mark of devotion he dedicated the Archaeological Museum to Pope Benedict XIV. Cardinal Stoppani gave the commission for the design of the Museum to the architect Giovan Battista Buonamici, who had already successfully designed the harbour of Pesaro in 1749. Up till 1819 the Museum was not subjected to any substantial modifications. It was only at the beginning of

Fragment of Section X: it represents the well-known episode of Ulysses and the Sirens.

the 20th century that some changes were made, such as the occupation of the ground-floor rooms in order to clear the courtyard. Though the transfer of the Museum to its new rooms had been carried out with the intention of permitting a future curator to maintain the same order as Buonamici, this did not in fact happen. For in 1944 the Museum was completely dismantled and transferred to the storerooms of the Ducal Palace, thus preventing it from being viewed and admired.

The present ring-like arrangement of the collection in the rooms of the Ducal Palace permits a thorough and rational view of the material on display. The Superintendency of Artistic and Historic Properties has also provided for the installation of thermohygrometric equipment to eliminate the possible risks which the display of such ancient artefacts might easily incur.

The existing layout of the Museum has retained its original subdivision into 22 sections, though some other material exists in addition to these, such as the wonderful fragments of sarcophagi datable to the mid-3rd century A.D.

Front of a funerary urn sculpted with a garland with two corner erotes placed at its ends. At the centre of the urn is the dedicatory inscription to T. Flavius Myrtilus Ianuarius, freedman of the Flavian house.

Some interesting fragments of ancient sarcophagi representing (inter alia) Eros and Psyche, the two famous Greek mythological figures who symbolise the eternal conflict between body and spirit, between sacred and profane love.

A relief depicting a lion being mauled by a dragon.

Visit to the monuments in the immediate vicinity of the Ducal Palace

Flanking the Ducal Palace on the Piazza Duca Federico is the *Cathedral* (or Duomo), whose left side delimits the piazza itself.

The building we now see dates to the late 18th century, and was designed in the neoclassical style by the architect Giuseppe Valadier (the façade, built out of Furlo stone is, however, the word of Camillo Morigia). It replaced a previous church built for Federico da Montefeltro by Francesco di Giorgio Martini which unfortunately collapsed as a result of the earthquake in 1789. Of this church in the Renaissance style some traces remain in the Chapel of the Sacrament. But nothing at all survives of the yet earlier church dating to the 11th century that already stood on the site, though this was in ruins prior to the construction of the 15th century edifice. The bell-tower, too, dates to the 18th century.

The Cathedral · façade.

The Cathedral · interior.

The Cathedral's interior clearly reveals the classicizing spirit of Valadier. Grand and solemn in its architectural style, it is notable for its spaciousness, elegance and nobility.

Various works of art are preserved in the church. Our tour begins from the right aisle.

Right aisle

1st altar: "Translation of the House of the Madonna" by C. Ridolfi.

2nd altar: "Martyrdom of St. Sebastian" by Federico Barocci, an interesting work by this painter of Urbino.

3rd altar: "St. Cecilia among Saints" by the same artist.

4th altar: "Crucifixion" by Viviani.

Right transept

Altar: "Madonna and Child with Saints" by Viviani.

Chapel of the Conception: it was decorated by Carlo Maratta, who also painted the altarpiece of the "Assumption of Mary". Traces of frescoes dating to the 14th century may also be noted.

Apse

The cupola is decorated with the figures of the Four Evangelists frescoed by various painters. Over the High Altar is a large painting by C. Unterberger (18th century) depicting the "Madonna assumed into heaven between Saints Crescentino and Mainardo" to whom the Cathedral is dedicated.

Left transept

Altar: statue of Clement XI by Cornacchini (18th century).

The Cathedral · interior:"Martyrdom of St. Sebastian" by Federico Barocci.

The Cathedral · Chapel of the Sacrament.

Chapel of the Sacrament: it is preceded by a handsome wrought-iron railing retrieved from the 15th century church destroyed by the earthquake. It contains one of Federico Barocci's finest paintings: "The Last Supper". The other painting of "The Institution of the Eucharist" is by Urbinelli.

Left aisle
4th altar: «Annunciation» by R. Motta.
3rd altar: «St. Charles» by C. Ridolfi.
2nd altar: «The Emperor Heraclius with the Cross» by Palma Giovane.
1st altar: «Visitation» by A. Viviani.

Before leaving the Cathedral we may find, adjacent to the Chapel of the Conception (in the right transept), the entrance to the Cathedral Museum or Albani Museum.

The Cathedral Museum or Albani Museum

It takes its name from its patron, Cardinal Annibale Albani, and contains works of art of various kind from a number of churches and convents in the town.

In the entrance hall are various preparatory sketches for the frescoes in the Cathedral.

1st Room (or Sacristy): here are displayed:
— a series of 14th and 15th century frescoes removed from the church of San Domenico.
— groups of ceramics.
— a beautiful terracotta statue of the Madonna (placed in a niche).

2nd Room: also known as the Room of the Treasury, because various sacred objects and church furnishings of great value are here assembled in a number of display-cases.
We may note in particular the magnificent collection of liturgical vestments, and the wonderful chalices studded with gems and precious stones. They belonged in large part to Cardinal Albani.

3rd Room: in this room too many precious objects are displayed in various vitrines. Particularly striking among them are the magnificent group of porcelain altar-ware (Saxon art of the 18th century), the ivory croziers, a pre-

Room of the Treasury.

"Madonna and Child" by Andrea Bologna.

cious Crucifix carved out of coral and a beautiful bronze lectern dating to the 13th century. The walls are hung with a number of paintings, some of them the work of the painter Masucci depicting "Scenes from the Life of St. Gregory".

4th Room: a number of paintings of some interest, but not all of certain attribution, are contained in this room. We may mention, among others, the works of Andrea Bologna (to whom a "Madonna and Child", also known as the "Madonna del Latte", is attributed). Federico Barocci ("The Blessed Michelina" and one or two other paintings, though in these the hand of his followers is prevalent), Timoteo Viti ("Adoration of Jesus"), Giovanni Santi ("St. Vincent"), Federico Zuccari ("Christ bound to the Column"), Giorgio Picchi and Battista Franco.

5th Room: this room, too, contains a number of paintings, of which we may mention the "Assumption of Mary with St. Crescentino" by Cialdieri, a beautiful "Madonna of Mercy" attributed by some to Girolamo Genga, a "Mary Magdalen" which some art historians consider to be by Guido Reni, and a "Madonna and Saints" by Antonio Palmerini.

6th Room: here are displayed many illuminated books with exquisitely painted miniatures, dating for the most part to the 14th and 15th century. Of great beauty is the bronze candelabrum sculpted with reliefs commemorating some events in the life of Duke Federico da Montefeltro; it has been attributed to the artist Francesco di Giorgio Mar-

"Madonna and Child" (known as the "Madonna of the Cat") Andrea Bologna

"Assumption with St. Crescentino" by Girolamo Cialdieri.

tini. The numismatic collection of Pope Clement XI is also of considerable interest and value.

To complete our tour of the Cathedral we should return outside and take a look at the right flank of the building. A portico erected in the 17th century to commemorate the marriage between Duke Federico Ubaldo della Rovere and Claudia dei Medici runs along it. It is from here that access is given to the *Crypt* of the Cathedral, consisting of several chapels. In one of these is located an interesting

"Nativity and Saints" by a follower of Timoteo Viti.

statue by Giovanni Bandini (16th century) representing the
«Dead Christ». One of these chapels is called the «Oratory
of the Grotto».
Let us now return once again to the Piazza Duca Federico,
and more precisely to the beginning of the adjacent Piazza
Rinascimento. Here stands the Church of San Domenico.

Church of San Domenico

Dating to the second half of the 14th century, the church is gothic in appearance. Its brick, gabled façade is preceded by a double stairway that converges on an elegant entrance door.

Commissioned by Duke Federico da Montefeltro, this portal, a distinguished example of the Renaissance style, was erected by Maso di Bartolomeo in the 15th century. A beautiful enamelled terracotta of the "Madonna and Child" by Luca della Robbia was once placed in the lunette over the doorway. It has now been removed to the Ducal Palace.

Church of San Domenico · portal of the façade by Maso di Bartolomeo.

The University · Main Hall.

The interior of the church consists of a single nave re-modelled by the architect Filippo Barigioni in the 18th century. It contains fine altarpieces by Francesco Vanni and Giovanni Conca.

Before leaving this centre of the civic life of Urbino to pursue our itinerary through the other districts of the town, we should take a look at one other building situated close to the Ducal Palace: this is the building housing the *University*, located at the end of the Piazza Rinascimento. This was in fact the residence of the Montefeltro family before the construction of the Ducal Palace. But of the original building little remains (we should note, in particular, the fine gothic portal), since it was almost totally re-constructed in the 17th century. Today, it is the seat of the University of Urbino which was founded in the early years of the 16th century. An inscription on the façade commemorates the fact that the celebrated 16th century Italian poet Torquato Tasso stayed here for some time as a guest of the lords of Urbino.

A tour of the town

Our visit to the rest of Urbino has two points of departure: the streets that fan out from the Piazza Rinascimento and reach the eastern and south-western area of the town, and those that depart from the Piazza della Repubblica.

1st itinerary
A) From the University to the church of Sant'Agostino and the Teatro Sanzio

From the University building at the foot of the Piazza Rinascimento we take the Via Saffi, flanked by ancient houses, which descends to the southern part of the town. On passing the small *church of Santa Caterina* behind the University (it contains paintings and stucco decorations by Federico Brandani), we continue down the Via Saffi, passing the *Palazzo Semproni* (15th century) and then the *church of San Paolo* of ancient origins but remodelled in the 17th century. A little further on, on the right-hand side of the street, is the *church of Sant'Agostino*.
It contains altarpieces by Claudio Ridolfi and Timoteo Viti. A 16th century sundial may also be noted.

At the bottom of the Via Saffi we may turn right into the street (the Via Matteotti) leading to the public gardens (the Pincio) laid out on the slopes of the hill and then (on the left) the Borgo Mercatale. After passing the latter, we come to the *Teatro Sanzio*: a mid-19th century theatre built by the architect Ghinelli. This is situated at a lower level than the twin-towered rear façade of the Ducal Palace, but at a higher level than the Piazza Mercatale, over which its rear extension stands.

In this part of the town we may also note the building known as the Data which contained the stables of the Ducal Palace and the ramp that connected them with the palace itself. Both were designed by Francesco di Giorgio Martini.

Of particular interest is the *spiral ramp*, i.e. the ramp which linked the parts of the palace we have just mentioned.

B) From the church of San Domenico to the convent of Santa Chiara

Taking the street (the Via di San Domenico) that runs along the side of the church of San Domenico (on the Piazza Rinascimento), we may first note the archaeological remains of the *Roman Theatre*, which have partly been recovered by excavation. We then come to the Piazza Gherardi with its handsome Palace of Justice (the former *Palazzo Gherardi* and an *aedicula* with frescoes by Ottaviano Nelli. To the left (on the Via di Ruscio) is the hand-

Spiral ramp by Francesco di Giorgio Martini.

some 15th century Renaissance-style *Palazzo Passionei*, while to the right the Via Santa Chiara leads to the *Convent of Santa Chiara* (St. Clare) designed by Francesco di Giorgio Martini and recently restored. Facing it, on the same street, is the *Oratory of the Holy Cross* which contains some interesting paintings by Ottaviano Nelli, Federico Zuccari, Urbinelli and Giovanni Santi.

Panel rappresenting the Confraternity of the Holy Cross exsisting since 1427

Oratory of Santa Croce.

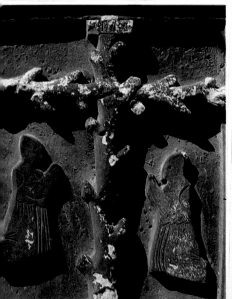

rom the Piazza della Repubblica to the western and northern area of the town.

From the Piazza Duca Federico we go down the Via Vittorio Veneto which brings us into the *Piazza della Repubblica*, the piazza that formed the ancient town centre before the Ducal Palace came to assume its role as the new focal point of the political and economic life of the town.

The piazza is situated in a kind of natural basin placed between the two hills on which Urbino stands. Fanning out from it are the various streets (four of them constituting the main thoroughfares of the ancient road system) that lead to the different districts of the town. By taking each of them in turn we may thus complete our tour of this wonderful town.

But before doing so, we should note, in the piazza itself, the *Palazzo Albani* and the *Collegio Raffaello* the former Renaissance in style and the latter erected by Pope Clement XI in the 18th century, with a portico in front; the school's pupils included the famous 19th century Italian poet Giovanni Pascoli.

Church of the Oratorio della Morte · "The Crucifixion · by Federico Barocci.

The Raffaello Sanzio Theatre · interior.

We are already familiar with the Via Vittorio Veneto which links the Piazza della Repubblica with the Ducal Palace. Along its course we may note a handsome stone arcade dating to the 15th century, the *Palazzo Municipale* (or Town Hall), distinguished on top by a glittering mosaic of the "Madonna and Child", and — by making a little detour by a side-road to the right — the *Oratorio della Morte*, an oratory which contains one of Federico Barocci's finest works: his painting of the "Crucifixion" over the high altar.

Returning to the Piazza della Repubblica, by taking the Via Garibaldi we may descend to the Teatro Sanzio and the eastern façade of the Ducal Palace.

The Via Battisti, which begins on the opposite side of the piazza, to the side of the Collegio Raffaello, leads to the stretch of town walls to the north-east of Urbino and to the town gate known as the Porta Lavagnine.

The Via Mazzini, in turn, leads off from the piazza in the opposite direction, leading to another town gate, the Porta Valbona (erected in the 17th century) and the Borgo Mercatale. Going down this street, we pass the *Palazzo Palma* which still preserves its handsome 15th century courtyard, the *Palazzo Luminati* (Renaissance in style) and lastly the church of *San Francesco di Paola*, built under the auspices of Duke Francesco Maria II Della Rovere at the beginning of the 17th century. Antonio Viviani was responsible for its magnificent interior decoration.

Almost opposite this church begins the *San Giovanni quarter*, which represents the oldest and most picturesque nucleus of medieval Urbino. Steep and characteristic stairways — the Scalette di San Giovanni — climb up the hill between ancient houses, opening up magnificent views over the older part of the town and the Ducal Palace beyond.

Oratory of San Giovanni Battista.

From here we may reach the *Oratory of San Giovanni Battista*, one of the town's most interesting monuments. Its construction dates to the last years of the 14th century (though its façade was rebuilt in recent times). What makes a visit to the oratory especially worthwhile is the wonderful cycle of frescoes that decorate its interior. These were largely executed by the brothers Jacopo and Lorenzo Salimbeni (1416). They constitute one of the greatest and most representative expressions of that late development of gothic art known as the International Gothic style, which was especially influenced by international trends and which differs from Italian gothic by its greater decorative richness, a more dazzling use of colour and a more subtle and elaborate use of line.

The cycle of frescoes narrates scenes from the life of St. John the Baptist, and entirely covers the walls of the church. We may also note a fine "Crucifixion" placed behind the high altar and the work of the same artists. Only a few of the frescoes belong to a slightly later period. The handsome wooden ceiling is also noteworthy.

Oratory of San Giovanni Battista · "The Baptism of Christ".

Apse wall with the "Crucifixion" by the Salimbeni brothers.

Frescoes of the life of St. John the Baptist:

Wall to the right, lower part: 1) St. John begins his preaching; 2) Baptism of new converts; 3) St. John baptises Jesus; 4) St. John rebukes Herod.

Wall to the left: apart from the remains of somewhat deteriorated frescoes by other painters, there are two further episodes from the life of St. John the Baptist: 1) The death of the Saint; 2) Deposition of St. John.

Not far from the Oratory of San Giovanni is the *Oratory of San Giuseppe*, a 16th century building which consists of a church in the baroque style (containing a large statue

Oratory of San Giuseppe · Crib by Federico Brandani.

of St. Joseph sculpted by Giuseppe Lironi and some paintings by Carlo Roncalli) and an adjoining chapel, in which
an original and extremely interesting *Crib* is preserved.
The work of Federico Brandani, this representation of the
manger in Bethlehem and the birth of Jesus is exquisitely
modelled in stucco and extremely realistic in its re-evocation of the event.

The same chapel also contains a fine marble bas-relief

of the "Madonna and Child" by Domenico Rosselli.

Before leaving the church, we should visit the Sacristy: it contains a noteworthy "Portrait of a Prelate" by Ghezzi and a series of fantastic landscapes painted on the cupboards which have been attributed to Salvator Rosa.

On leaving the Oratory of San Giuseppe, we return to the Piazza della Repubblica by going up the Via Barocci, one of the most characteristic and evocative streets in the town due to the medieval atmosphere that permeates it and that distinguishes, in an unmistakable way, its houses and the whole district around it.

Here, in the midst of ancient houses and picturesque al-

Church of San Francesco.

Chapel with the "Pietà".

leyways, we may also find the *Barocci House:* the house in which the painter Federico Barocci was born — one of Urbino's most illustrious sons and an artist whose works we have been able to admire in the course of our visits to the various buildings described in this guide.

On returning to the Piazza della Repubblica, we now turn into the last of the streets leading off from it: the Via Raffaello which represents another itinerary of considerable interest. At the beginning of the street, to the right, we may note the *church of San Francesco*; remodelled in the 18th century, it retains from the original 17th century building an elegant portal and a handsome bell-tower.

The interior consists of a very wide nave and two aisles. It was reconstructed in the 18th century, but its floor preserves many earlier tomb-slabs of distinguished citizens of Urbino. Particularly noteworthy is the *Chapel of the Sacrament* (to the right of the sanctuary), formerly the chapel of the Della Rovere Dukes and thus dating back to the original nucleus of the church. We should note in particular its large marble arch richly decorated with bas-reliefs by Costantino Trappola. A similar arch is situated in the chapel to the left of the apse in which a stone "Pietà" placed over the remains of a sarcophagus may also be admired. In the apse is a large painting by Federico Barocci ("Forgiveness of St. Francis") and, in the third altar on the left, the remains of a fresco of the "Crucifix" of the school of Salimbeni. Two 15th century stone sarcophagi are situated at the beginning of the nave.

Fountain in front of the Palazzo Albani (18th century).   **Statue of Pope Clement XI.**

On leaving the church, we continue our way up the Via Raffaello. If we like, we can make a detour to the right by taking the Via Bramante, another of the characteristic streets of Urbino; along its course we may find a charming 18th century *fountain*, the house in which Pope Clement XI was born, and the interesting *Botanic Gardens*, containing a wealth of meticulously selected plants. Just after it is the *church of Santo Spirito* (with an elegant portal) and a series of 15th and 16th century houses belonging to families of local artists. At the bottom of the Via Bramante, we come to one of the gates in the town walls: the 17th century *Porta di Santa Lucia* which commands fine panoramic views of the town.

We then resume our exploration of the Via Raffaello, which ascends at a measured pace towards the top of one of the hills on which Urbino is built. We soon come, on the left, to one of the most significant and important buildings for the history and art of Urbino: namely

The House of Raphael

The painter Raphael Sanzio was in fact born in this

house in 1483. His father was Giovanni Santi, he too a painter, though on a far more modest scale, numerous of whose works may still be seen in the town. It was from him that Raphael learnt the rudiments of painting, before being apprenticed to Timoteo Viti. At an early age he went to Perugia where he became a pupil of Pietro Vannucci (better known as Perugino). Later, in 1506, he went to Florence where he came into contact with the art of great masters like Leonardo and Michelangelo. Extraordinarily precocious, Raphael soon became famous and sought

Genealogical tree in the House of Raphael.

after in various courts, and was called to Rome to see to the decoration of the Vatican *Stanze*: a commission entrusted to him by Pope Julius II on the recommendation of the architect Bramante. He died in Rome in 1520 — at the age of 37 — after having also assumed the direction of the project for the building of the new basilica of St. Peter. All his paintings are suffused by an unmistakable grace and delicacy, and it may be affirmed that Raphael was one of the most significant interpreters of the ideal of beauty and perfection exemplified by the art of the Renaissance.

A visit to Raphael's house is worthwhile not only on account of the several paintings it contains (though

Kitchen in the House of Raphael.

Raphael's masterpieces are mainly to be found in the cities in which he did most of his works, i.e. Florence and Rome), but also because it provides a very clear and evocative idea of what a typical 15th century house was like. At the present time, the Raphael Academy is housed on the second floor.

Our visit begins on the ground floor where, beyond a charming little courtyard, we may enter two rooms of modest dimensions but very evocative in mood. We may note in particular the *kitchen* with its ancient fireplace and various period furnishings. Noteworthy, too, in this room is the rustic, wooden-beamed ceiling, and the ingenious re-

volving spit over the fireplace.

From the ticket office where we may admire a fine stone bas-relief which almost certainly comes from the nearby house of Bramante, we may proceed to a visit to the apartment proper on the first floor:

1st Room or Raphael's Room; the room in which, according to tradition, the painter was born. The works of art dis-

Stone bas-relief by Bramante.

played here include the following:
— predella by Berto di Giovanni, a copy of the one painted by Raphael
— "Moses saved from the waters", a pen and ink sketch with Raphael's own signature
— genealogical tree of the Sanzio family
— "Madonna and Child", one of Raphael's earliest works in fresco.

"Madonna with Child", one of Raffaello's very first fresco works (recently restored)

2nd Room (Sala Grande): this handsome large room has an elegant fireplace and a fine wooden coffered ceiling. It contains three copies of famous paintings by Raphael:
— "The Madonna of the Chair"
— "The Madonna of the Goldfinch"
— "The Vision of Ezechiel"
— "Annunciation" by Raphael's father, Giovanni Santi
— "Madonna and Child" Giulio Romano
— "Pietà" by Raphael's master, Timoteo Viti.

House of Raphael · Entrance hall.

3rd Room or Bedroom of Giovanni Saint: of the various works displayed in this room we may mention the "Coronation of the Virgin" (interesting painting by Orlando Merlini) and "Saints Peter and Paul" (by a Flemish master).

Having visited the apartment on the first floor, we may then ascend to the second floor, on which the already mentioned Raphael Academy has its seat and where other paintings by various artists and a series of mementoes of, and records and books about, the great artist of Urbino are

"Coronation of the Virgin" by Orlando Merlini.

on display.

The stone on which Giovanni Santi ground his paints may still be seen in the charming little inner courtyard of the house.

On leaving Raphael's house, we note, immediately afterwards, on the same side of the street, the ancient *church of San Sergio*; though 15th century in its present appearance, it was in fact founded in the 6th century. Its interior contains paintings by Ridolfi, Cialdieri and Nelli, Archaeological remains of the Roman period were also uncovered during restoration of its floor.

Continuing up the Via Raffaello, we may note the fine Renaissance arcade of the *Old Hospital* and then, at the end of the street, close to the walls, the so-called "Giro del Cassero" begins to the right; it leads through the bastions and through the old "borgo".

Stone on which Giovanni Santi ground his paints.

SU QUESTA PIETRA
VENIVANO MACINATI I
COLORI NELLA BOTTEGA
DI GIOVANNI SANTI

Walks outside the walls

At the end of the Via Raffaello beyond the ramparts by which Urbino is surrounded, is the large square formed by the Piazzale Roma, in which the *Monument to Raphael Sanzio* is situated. It was sculpted by Luigi Belli. Significant episodes from the life and work of the artist are sculpted in bas-relief on its pedestal. The two statues

Monument to Raphael Sanzio.

War Memorial.

flanking the monument represent "Renascence" and "Genius".

Other statues of famous artists and personages born in or associated with Urbino are placed here and there under the trees.

From this point we can enjoy extensive panoramic views over the town and the nearby hills.

Not very far from the Piazzale Roma is the *Fortezza dell'Albornoz*, a massive 15th century fortress now in the process of being restored. It was built by Cardinal Albornoz when Urbino was subjected to the rule of the Papal State.

From this position too — we are standing on the highest hill of the town — we can enjoy magnificent, sweeping panoramic views.

Not far from the Fortezza Albornoz is situated the Monument to the fallen in both world wars, a striking sculpture in iron.

Of the sights worth visiting on the outskirts of Urbino, one that should not be missed is the *church of San Bernardino* which is situated close to the Cemetary. It is also known as the Mausoleum of the Dukes, because the Dukes of Montefeltro, Federico and Guidobaldo, were buried here.

Elegance, simplicity and sobriety are the distinguishing features of this building, both outside and inside. The harmoniousness and perfect proportions of its architectural forms (the church dates to the late 15th century) have led to its being attributed to the architect Francesco di Giorgio Martini; other scholars have also recognised the hand of Bramante in it. Adjoining the church, we may admire the very simple but evocative cloisters. At their centre is a well-head bearing, above, the symbol of the Franciscan order.

Church of San Bernardino · Tomb of Federico da Montefeltro.

Cloisters of San Bernardino.

Another agreeable walk can be made to the top of the little hill known as the *Colle dei Cappuccini* outside the Porta Valbona, where it is possible to visit the charming little church of the Capuchins, an oasis of tranquillity set amid a landscape of cypresses.

From the top of this hill, our glance can take in the whole of "windy Urbino", just as the Italian poet Pascoli did. He wrote a famous poem about it.

A further walk takes us through the modern suburbs of Urbino (from the Porta Santa Lucia) to the *church of the Annunciata*, with a fine interior decorated with altarpieces and frescoes by Antonio Viviani and Ottaviano Nelli. We may then continue our walk as far as the *church of the Madonna dell'Homo*, in which frescoes of some value, painted by Ottaviano Nelli in the 15th century, are preserved.

The Feast of the Duke

A town like Urbino which boasts of so ancient and illustrious a history; a town whose artistic splendour is rivalled by few other cities in Italy and has always placed it on the highest cultural levels in the past and the present; a town renowned for the magnificence of its traditions — such a town, in short, could not fail to re-evoke, like many other historic centres in the peninsula, the sum of its customs, its heritage, its most significant events and its illustrious men.

Here too, therefore, the so-called "Feast of the Duke" has been held since 1981; it includes a jousting competition and a historic parade in period costumes. This fascinating event is annually held in August and is aimed at commemorating and re-evoking personages from Urbino's past, the most significant events in the history of the ancient Duchy, aspects of the town's social, artistic and economic life, and local traditions and customs.

The event has justly been called the "Feast of the Duke" to honour the man who was, above all others, the creator of Urbino; the man who established its power, promoted its beauty and ensured its historic importance and continuing fame right down to our own days: Federico da Montefeltro.

The programme varies each year, at least as regards the re-evocation of the illustrious personage after whom it is named. Yet in general outline the celebration remains al-

Historic Procession.

FOTO A. DI PAOLI

Historic Procession.

most unchanged from year to year. It begins in the morning with the Reading of the Proclamation announcing the event. In the afternoon, the representation in costume of the historic re-evocation already mentioned is performed. This is followed by the Jousting Competition (or Knightly Tourney of the Courtiers, as it is called), which consists of a contest between horsemen from various Italian cities. It takes the form of trying on horseback to pierce a ring attached to a support. The group that scores the highest number of points is awarded the Banner (the *Palio*) of the town for that year.

The day's celebrations end in the early evening with the Historic Procession: a magnificent and evocative parade of men and women dressed in period costumes, who represent the dukes, the nobles, the knights, the prelates, the soldiers and the people of those times. The procession is enlivened by the brilliant colours, velvets and silks of the costumes, of the greatest effect.

The festivity is accompanied by a series of other events, such as the displays of the flag-wavers, and the musicians who perform on clarions and drums.

Everything concurs to re-evoke the splendour of the ancient Court of Urbino and the social and cultural traditions with which it is inseparably linked.

Useful information

Azienda di Soggiorno e Turismo
Piazza Rinascimento, 1 - Tel. 26.13

Azienda di Soggiorno e Turismo
Piazza Duca Federico, 35 -
Tel. 24.41

A.C.I.
Automobile Club d'Italia
Piazza Casteldurante, 27 -
Tel. 25.97

Touring Club Italiano (T.C.I.)
Ufficio Succursale
Piazza Rinascimento, 7 - Tel. 25.88

Ufficio Viaggi «APATAM»
Via Mazzini, 98 - Tel. 4731 - 329488
Telex 560690

Ufficio Viaggi «Marcionni»
Biglietteria Ferroviaria
Ufficio Cambio
Via Puccinotti, 7
Tel. 328877 TELEX n. 581018

Ufficio Viaggi «Ulysses' Travel»
Biglietteria ferroviaria
Ufficio Cambio
Via Mazzini, 22/24
Tel. 41.73 (3 Linee Urbane)
TELEX n. 561015

Centro Organizzazione Congressi
Urbino Meetings
Via San Domenico, 1
Tel. 328877
Telex 561018

Agenzia Immobiliare Feltresca
Via V. Veneto, 10 - Tel. 2226

Agenzia «Quadrifoglio»
Pratiche Universitarie e
Automobilistiche
Via C. Battisti, 14 - Tel. 24.34

Banca Nazionale del Lavoro
Ufficio Cambio
Via V. Veneto, 58 - Tel. 32.86.58

Banca Popolare di Ancona
Ufficio Cambio - Bancomat
Viale Comandino - Tel. 32.93.58

Cassa di Risparmio di Pesaro
Ufficio Cambio - Bancomat
Via V. Veneto, 47 - Tel. 32.93.92

Palazzo Ducale
Sovraintendenza per i Beni
Artistici e Storici delle Marche
Piazza Rinascimento, 13
Tel. 27.60 - 320315

Sezione Archivio di Stato
Via V. Veneto, 42 - Tel. 26.21

Osservatorio Meteorologico
«A. Serpieri» - Tel. 41.66

Università degli Studi - Sede
centrale
Via Saffi, 2
Centralino Telefonico 30.51
Corsi Estivi per Stranieri
Segreteria Tel. 45.11
Biblioteca - Via Saffi, 2 - Tel. 45.11

Centro Alti Studi Europei
(C.A.S.E.)
Segreteria Tel. 320005
Via Saffi, 1

Sogesta - Centro Studi
Località Crocicchia
Direzione e Ufficio - Tel. 3001
Centro Residenziale - Tel. 329888

Accademia Raffaello
Centro Internazionale Artistico
Culturale
Via C. Battisti, 54 - Tel. 329695

Ispettorato Distrettuale delle
Foreste
Via G. Dini, 18 - Tel. 328931

Stazione Autocorriere
Borgo Mercatale - Tel. 28.26
(Bar Europa)

Taxi
Piazza Della Repubblica -
Tel. 25.50

Ufficio Postale e Telegrafico
Informazioni - Tel. 25.75
Via Bramante, 18

Posti Telefonici Pubblici:
Piazza Rinascimento, 4
- Piazza San Francesco
- Centro Promozionale Pubblicità
Via Budassi, 6 - Tel. 41.31
- Bari Vito
Via Mazzini, 36 - Tel. 26.19
- Big Ben Sala Attrazioni
Corso Garibaldi, 29 - Tel. 32.96.20

Ospedale Civile
Centralino - Tel. 329351-328121-
328122
Via B. Da Montefeltro

Croce Rossa Italiana
Via dei Morti - Tel. 329.518

Farmacia Comunale
Viale Comandino, 41 - Tel. 329189

Farmacia Centrale
Piazza della Repubblica, 9 -
Tel. 329829

Farmacia Nuova
Via Raffaello, 25 - Tel. 320031

Farmacia Lucciarini
Corso Garibaldi, 12 - Tel. 27.81

Farmacia Ricciarelli
Via Mazzini, 2 - Tel. 28.08

Erboristeria «Tre Streghe»
Via dei Fornari, 7

Albergo Diurno - Via C. Battisti, 2

**Commissariato della
Polizia di Stato**
Borgo Mercatale, 15
Tel. 27.25-28.96

Soccorso Pubblico di Emergenza
Tel. 113

Soccorso A.C.I. - Tel. 116

Pronto Intervento - Tel. 112

Carabinieri
Viale Comandino, 1
Comando Compagnia -
Tel. 328821
Comando Stazione - Tel. 328822

Giardia di Finanza
Via Bramante, 21 - Tel. 28.20

Polizia Stradale
Via Sasso, 78/B - Tel. 328225

Vigili del Fuoco
Via G. da Montefeltro, 33 - Tel. 115

Vigili Urbani
Piazza della Repubblica, 3 -
Tel. 26.45 - 32.04.91

Alberghi - Pensioni

**** Bonconte
Via delle Mura, 28 -
Tel. 2463 - 4782

*** Fontespino
Via Nazionale, 73/Bis
Tel. 57190 - 57160 Km. 4,5

*** Montefeltro
Via Piansevero, 2
Tel. 328324 - 328325

*** La Meridiana
Via Cal Biancone, 154/A
Loc. Trasanni Km. 3
Tel. 320169

*** Piero della Francesca
Viale Comandino, 53
Tel. 328427 - 328428

*** Raffaello
Via S. Margherita, 38/40 -
Tel. 4784 - 4896

*** Residence
Via Giannetto Dini, 12
Tel. 328227 - 328009 -
328226

** Due Querce
Via Stazione, 35
Tel. 2509 - 4700

** Italia
Corso Garibaldi, 32
Tel. 2701

** La Muta
Loc. Castelcavallino
Str. Feltresca, 171/A
Tel. 349131 Km. 6

** San Giovanni
Via Barocci, 13 - Tel. 2827

** Panoramic
Via Nazionale, 192
Tel. 2600

P* Feltria
Via G. Da Montefeltro, 18
Tel. 328178

— Casa dello studente
Piazza S. Filippo - Tel. 2935

— Casa della studentessa
Via Pozzo Nuovo, 1
Tel. 4097

**— Collegio Maestre Pie
Venerini**
Via Muzio Oddi
Tel. 328585

— Collegi Universitari
Colle dei Cappuccini
Tel. 327041 - 328242 -
329251

— Istituto S. Felicita
Via del Fiancale, 1
Tel. 2815

**— Pension. «Maria
Immacolata»**
Via Mazzini, 36 - Tel. 2853

— Casa di Accoglienza
Canonica di S. Sergio
Via Raffaello, 59 - Tel. 2532

— Campeggio «Pineta»
M.D. Cesana (S. Donato -
Km. 2) Tel. 4710

Ristoranti - Trattorie - Pizzerie - Paninoteche

Ristorante «Bramante»
Via Bramante, 54 - Tel. 2676

Ristorante «Da Bruno»
Via V. Veneto, 45 - Tel. 2598

Ristorante «Nuovo Coppiere»
Via Porta Maja, 20 - Tel. 320092

Ristorante «Il Cortegiano»
Via Puccinotti, 13 - Tel. 320307

Ristorante Pizzeria «Europa»
Borgo Mercatale, 22 - Tel. 2826

Ristorante «Taverna La Fornarina»
Via Mazzini, 14 - Tel. 320007

Ristorante «Fosca»
Via Budassi, 64 - Tel. 2521

**Ristorante Pizzeria
«San Giovanni»**
Via Barocci, 13 - Tel. 2286

Ristorante «La Meridiana»
Loc. Trasanni Km. 3
Via Cal Biancone, 54/A -
Tel. 320169

Ristorante «Montefeltro»
Via Piansevero, 2
Tel. 328324-328325

Ristorante «Munari»
Loc. Pantiere Km. 10 - Tel. 580400

Ristorante «La Muta»
Strada Feltresca, 171
Loc. Castelcavallino Km. 6
Tel. 349131

Ristorante «Pasta à Gogo»
Via Valerio, 16 - Tel. 2942

Ristorante «Piazzetta delle erbe»
Piazza San Francesco, 6 -
Tel. 4894

Ristorante «Vecchia Urbino»
Via Vasari, 3/5 - Tel. 4447

Ristorante «NE NÈ»
Via Crocicchia, 30 - Tel. 2996

Ristorante «Ragno D'Oro»
Piazzale Roma (apertura estiva)

Ristorante «VIP»
Via Nazionale Bocca Trabaria, 4
Tel. 4075

Ristorante Self-Service «Franco»
Via del Poggio, 1 - Tel. 2492

Ristorante Pizzeria «Fontespino»
Via Nazionale 73 bis Km. 4,5 -
Tel. 57190-57160

Ristorante Pizzeria «Il Giardino»
Via Pallino, 46 - Km. 4 - Tel. 328919

Ristorante Pizzeria «La Cometa»
Via G. da Montefeltro, 7 -
Tel. 328606

**Ristorante Pizzeria
«La Vecchia Miniera»**
Loc. La Miniera Km. 10 - Tel. 55229

Ristorante Pizzeria «Le Cesane»
Località S. Maria delle Selve
Km 6 (apertura estiva)

Ristorante Pizzeria «Da Vanda»
Loc. Castelcavallino Km. 8 -
Tel. 349117

Taverna «Zuzzurellone»
Via Cesare Battisti, 35

Trattoria «Del Leone»
Via C. Battisti, 5 - Tel. 329894

Trattoria - Pizzeria «Anita»
Loc. Gadana Km. 4 - Tel. 328150

Pizzeria «Zi Mari»
Loc. Montesoffio Km. 8 - Via
Nazionale, 73 bis - Tel. 57105

**Pizzeria Tavola Calda «La
Rustica»**
Via Nuova, 3 - Tel. 2528

**Pizzeria Tavola Calda «Le Tre
Piante»**
Via Foro Posterula, 1 - Tel. 4863

Pizzeria tavola calda «Rinascita»
Piazza Casteldurante, 2/4

Tavola Calda
Corso Garibaldi, 23 - Tel. 2229

Rosticceria «Il Girarrosto»
Piazza San Francesco, 3 -
Tel. 4445

Rosticceria «Mille Voglie»
Via G. da Montefeltro - Tel. 327121

Rosticceria
Via Santa Margherita, 11

Agrituristica «L'Aquilone»
Cà Palmiere Montesoffio Km. 7 -
Tel. 57107 - 57146 (apertura estiva)

Agriturismo «Beaty Farm»
Loc. Pozzuolo, 60 - Km. 9
Tel. 57183

Agrituristica «Trelaghi»
Pantiere, n. 6 - Km. 10 - Tel. 580455

Paninoteca «Lo sfizio»
Via V. Veneto, 19

Agripan
Via del Leone, 11 - Tel. 327448

Teatri - Cinema - Dancings

Teatro Sanzio
Corso Garibaldi - Tel 2281

Cinema Teatro Ducale
Via Budassi - Tel. 2413

Supercinema
Via T. Viti - Tel. 320051

Cinema Nuova Luce
Via Veterani

Discoteca «Club 83»
Via Nuova, 4 - Tel. 2512

Discoteca «Scorpio»
Via Nazionale 73/Bis - Tel. 2400

Associazioni culturali

Accademia Raffaello
Via Raffaello, 57 - Tel. 320105

Italia Nostra
Piazza Rinascimento, 7 - Tel. 2588

World Wildlife (WWF)
Piazza Rinascimento, 1

Dialettale Urbinate
Via M.L. King, 5 - Tel. 4226

Cappella Musicale
Via Valerio, 7 - Tel. 4120

Centro Sperimentale Teatrale Teatro Cust
Castelcavallino, 213 - Tel. 349183

Circolo Acli
Via S. Chiara, 19 - Tel. 2567

Circolo Universitario
Piazza S. Filippo - Tel. 2609

Associazione Studenti Esteri Italiani
Via S. Chiara, 19 - Tel. 2567

Circolo Arci
Via Pozzo Nuovo, 23 - Tel. 2431

Circolo cittadino
Piazza della Repubblica - Tel. 2936

Associazioni sportive

Circolo sportivo calcio «Montefeltro»
Via SS. Annunziata - Tel. 328167

Tennis (A.T.P.)
Via SS. Annunziata - Tel. 327380

Tennistavolo
Via Pozzo Nuovo, 6 - Tel. 327338

Centro sportivo universitario «Cus»
Via N. Sauro, 12 - Tel. 4893

Moto club «F. da Montefeltro»
Via Pablo Neruda - Tel. 327008

Polisportiva «Robur Tiboni»
Piazza della Repubblica

Società gruppo tiro a volo «Montefeltro»
Via Bocca Trabaria, n. 67
Tel. 329560

Associazione aquilonistica «AUDA»
«Le Aquile di Urbino»
Collegio Raffaello - Tel. 329930

Impianti sportivi

Stadio comunale «Montefeltro»
Via SS. Annunziata - Tel. 328696

Piscina palestra coperta «F.lli Cervi»
Loc. Varea - Tel. 329045

Piscina coperta (I.S.E.F.)
Via SS. Annunziata - Tel. 328312

Bocciodromo Comunale «Montefeltro»
Loc. Varea - Tel. 328055

Campo di Tiro a volo
Loc. Mondolce

Campi da Tennis
- Via Nazionale, 73/Bis
- Via SS. Annunziata - Tel. 327380
- Colle dei Cappuccini

Palestra di Judo - Karate
Via San Bartolo

Club Ippico «Le Cesane»
Loc. S. Maria delle Selve
Monte della Cesana - Tel. 340171

BY KIND PERMISSION OF THE AZIENDA DI SOGGIORNO E TURISMO OF URBINO

1   **Ducal Palace**
    National Gallery of the
    Marche
2   **Metropolitan Basilica**
3   **University of Urbino**
4   **Church of San Domenico**
5   **Egyptian Obelisk**
6   **Remains of Roman Theatre**
7   **Former Convent of Santa Chiara**

8   **Oratorio della Morte**
9   **Church of San Francesco**
10 **Church of the Madonna dell'Homo**
11 **Oratory of San Giuseppe**
12 **Raphael's Birth House**
13 **Monument to Raphael**
14 **Albornoz Fortress**
15 **Oratory of San Giovanni**

16 Teatro Sanzio

17 Church of the Cappuccini

18 Church of San Bernardino
Mausoleum of the Dukes

19 Albani Museum

20 Porta Valbona

21 Synagogue

22 Oratory of Santa Croce

23 Church of San Paolo,

24 Church of Sant'Agostino

25 Church of San Sergio

26 Church of Santo Spirito

27 Church of the Scalzi

28 Church of the Cinque
Piaghe

29 Helicoidal ramp

30 Plasters Museum

INDEX

© Copyright by Casa Editrice Plurigraf
S.S. Flaminia, km 90 - 05035 Narni - Terni - Italia
Tel. 0744 / 715946 - Fax 0744 / 722540 - (Italy country code: +39)
Tutti i diritti riservati. Riproduzione anche parziale vietata.
Stampa: 1995 - Plurigraf S.p.A. - Narni

L. 6.000
I.V.A. INCLUSA